BEASTIES, BIRDS, AND BELLES

A Poetry Collection

Orla Jane Drummond

AOS Publishing, 2025

Copyright © 2025

Orla Jane Drummond

ISBN: 978-1-998662-71-5

Cover Design: Meredith Lindsay

Visit AOS Publishing's website:
www.aospublishing.com

For Mamie-

Poetry is music and these songs are for you.

Contents

INTRODUCTION

I don't recall what the first poem I ever read was.
It's hard to imagine a time when I wasn't reading,
Shakespeare's plays and sonnets were an early love
and spending time with the Brontë sisters and the dark
musings of Poe are ripe sources for any young
person's imagination.

However, when I grew up and wished to place my own
prose on the page, there was one bard above all the
others that I wished to revisit. In Scotland, we study
the poems of Rabbie Burns from early childhood and
celebrate his life and work on the twenty-fifth of
January every year.
"'Tae a Mouse'" was always my favourite and it is from
the poem's titular mouse that I drew the 'beastie' part
of this book's title.

My home city, Glasgow, with its storied industrial
history, is also home to several fine green spaces,
which any artist would have no trouble connecting
with. From there, inspiration flourished and I wished
to look at the small things in nature, the overlooked in
the everyday; there's blossoms aplenty and the weather
is always changing.
Birds, especially, have always been very dear to me
and it is lucky for me that the word serves as a double
entendre (in Scotland and other places 'bird' can also
refer to a woman).

They're as rich in symbolism as they are in beauty and through them, I delve into themes of spiritualism and human nature.

Finally, the 'belles' refer to those incomprehensibly ethereal women of fiction, myth, and fables; demure maidens and divine Goddesses who have fascinated me all my life.

The one exception to the short form poetry, is the very last one in the group; which is an imagined debate between Athena, Goddess of Wisdom and Strategy and her brother, Ares, the God of War.
The subject of war and the needless destruction of human lives was in the back of my mind while writing about precious things in nature; I couldn't help but wonder how two patron deities might discuss their roles amongst themselves.
Ultimately, I concluded that neither is superior than the other, where their "art" is concerned.

This short collection is a musing on life and a celebration of many things that I love deeply and spend many a night pondering.
I hope, dear reader, whomever you may be, that you find it to your liking.

BEASTIES

MIDGE

You bury yourself under my skin.
You swarm me, irritate me;
Endless torment in the endless heat.
Vicious creature, a glutton for blood-
I will know peace at last when you are gone.

SNAILTRAIL

Looping, swirling, turning,
Quizzical, curious, opaque.
Temporary artform.
A journey taken.
Unknown artist, unique artisté.

MOLLUSK

Scrumptious oddity.
Poor man's feast, fit for a royal table.
I like you best with a sparkling wine,
There is no better partner with which to dine.

BLUEBOTTOM

Droning, frittering, noisy creature!
In my business, in my lunch.
Revoltingly gorgeous.
With a strange sheen of azure hue.
You fly around at your leisure.

ODE TO A HONEYBEE

Oh, sweet Honeybee, how your gentle kiss stings as you part from me.
Oh darling Damselfly, you would flit into the river rather than stay by my side.
Oh, brilliant Firefly, you burn so bright as you say your goodbyes.
On your head sits a crown of dross and gold brocade.
Obereon's muse would be your envy if you fancied anything but your own fair face.
Oh, precious Mayfly, let the day pass and go away from me.
Only I, alone, wish to be.

HIVE

Punch in for the day and off you go:
Delivering goods, returning home.
Feed the young and tend to the old.
Give reverence to the powers that be.
Buzz with the girls as you work on the line.
Flowers when you're born and flowers when you die.
Even when you're gone, there will always be a hive.

NECTAR

Pour me a glass of the sweet stuff;
The evening is young and our rendezvous is just
beginning.
Honey, I love you, every time.
Won't you call my bluff?

MRS SPIDER

Hey there, Mrs Spider,
Up there on the ceiling.
Are you lonely on this cold night?

Hey there, Mrs Spider.
Your threads drape all about you-
Has anyone told you how pretty they are?

Hey there, Mrs Spider.
There's so much I want to ask you.
Are you proud of the home you've made?

Hey there, Mrs Spider.
I heard you were a king-maker.
Did anyone thank you?
Or did they only think of him?

Hey there, Mrs Spider.
Soon it will be morning.
Your children will leave you with the rising sun.

Hey there, Mrs Spider.
Your babies have all gone now.
Was it worth it?
Such a short little life.

Hey there, Mrs Spider.
There's no one around to mourn you,
But I'll be thinking of you.
'Till the day I die.

STAG

White Stag, Red Stag,
Tussling in the snow.
A doe for the victor;
Food for the champion.
Through beauty and violence,
Does life continue to grow?

ROADKILL

Cracked snails and broken starlings.
Trampled foxes and crushed voles.
Smashed worms and startled rabbits.
There is little time given to you, in the bitter light of
day—
A minor inconvenience until someone sweeps you
away.
You weigh heavily on my afternoons when I pass you
on the road.
I'm sure some kinder soul than I would bury you.
This small obituary is my offering to the gentle
deceased.

BIRDS

A FINCH SINGS

A finch sings on a summer's night,
Perched on high, feathers kissed by the dying light,
From the garden, I watch you, your song caged in
barbed wire.
What is it about you that Darwin so admired?
Behind you, great buildings tower and loom in ashen
clouds.
Tell me, little finch, where on Earth will you go?
From the garden, I cannot reach you as the night
creeps in.
Your song is finished now.
Will I ever hear it again?
A finch falls silent on a summer's night,
And fire, made by man's hands, sets the sky alight.

DOVE OF PEACE

Why do we cling to dreams of winged doves?
Of an afterlife, of loved ones looking down upon us
from above?
We sit in metal houses and agonise over whether
we're special or whether our lives have any meaning.
We build rockets and send them into space, traverse
every inch of the land and sea,
But when the sun comes down, we are all children;
We fear the dark and craft artificial suns to light our
homes.
Death follows us everywhere and we fight tooth and
nail to leave some small trace behind.
We stomp our feet and scream ourselves hoarse to
make ourselves be seen.
Men in glass towers play games with lives before
afternoon tea.
In a world with no justice, what else is there to hope
for the love of the divine?
I do not think I shall be a sheep at the world's end.
But God would weep, I think, to see what they have
left for us.

PIGEONS OF CALPE

The plazas and the waterways are where we make
our home.
Tourists snap at us and throw us their scraps.
In the apartments above our streets where
holidaymakers reside, our cousins roost.
Parrots and canaries and cockatoos sleep on the
balconies.
We rest on the cafe roofs, the gutters above the
pharmacy and supermarket.
Athletes and sailors and pilgrims of faiths all stop to
chase us or toss us some crumbs.
Our hometown is teeming with history and against
the sun, the great rock looms.
As the ships return to the harbour, we fight seagulls
for the catch of the day.
We linger in the old town and follow as the autobus
circles its route for the dozenth time today.
Pigeons are alike all over but through a camera's
lens, they are most special in Calpe.

MAGPIE

A rhyme from my childhood.
Jackdaw coat of hidden rainbows.
Laughing bird of luck and sorrow.
You litter the pavements and illuminate the woods,
A flock as gorgeous as you are misunderstood.

CROW

Old friend, clever corvid,
Bird of fancy and sharp break,
Let the others keep their bright plumes.
What's a menagerie compared to splendorous
solitude?

KINGFISHER

Splendid highness,
Rarity of the river,
To glimpse your entourage.
Is worth the crown jewels.
And all of life's pleasures.

GUGA

Seabird, delicacy,
Creature of a culture I do not know.
Cha toil leam guga,
I wish I could say.
For as long as I have this plain tongue of mine,
Your taste shall remain unknown.

BLOSSOMS

MONKSHOOD

To think I would find something familiar at the side
of this strange, winding thoroughfare.
I scarcely noticed at first—that unmistakable purple
caress.
Little wayfarer, well covered for the rainfall.
Do you gather in a circle to pray, like the men of
cloth for whom you're named?
Do you pray at all, or do you simply be?
Beautiful flower with poison in your leaves,
You ensnared my interest long ago, though I'm
happiest to watch you from afar.
A kiss from you would lull me to sleep forever.
I can only watch you while I'm awake.
Safe travels, hooded traveller, the fields are wide and
dense.
The rain is lighter now.
'Till we meet again, my deathly friend.

TULIPS

Petals of a thousand colours,
Girls of the wind and summer air,
Men have been driven mad to possess you.
I prefer you in a neighbouring garden—
To see but never to take.

SNOWDROP

Winter's End—
First sign of hope.
One little drop of a wish.
My birthday bouquet, I'll have no other.
White doves on green stems,
You fade as quickly as you grace us.
By year's beginning, you'll come again.

GOOSEBERRY

Gooseberry green,
Those eyes that turn sour and sweet,
A delicious treat to taste.
Mouse's delight, to be hidden in the pantry—
A forbidden feast.
Mine alone.

FLYTRAP

To meet my last in your pretty jaws;
There would be no nicer fate.
Sing something jaunty as I fall down your throat.
This will be a nice story to share after dinner.

OAK

Stalwart, unflinching,
A home for small things.
A fine countertop.
Seeds for a forest.
Wood for a chair.
Decorative lifeline.

APPLE

Bite once for wisdom.
Bite twice for flavour.
Bite three times for bitterness.
Bite the core for tragedy.

LILACS

To the maiden with the lilacs in her hair:
Your tender touch, it rends the earth bare.
You wade in mist and waltz in shadows.
On rainy days, I see you there, reclining in your
loamy hollow.
You whisper to the ground and your voice is lost to
the wind.
The tendrils of melody reach me, and I hear you
sing.
Are you lonely in the corner of that great, unknowing
eye?
Or are you content to sit and watch eternity pass you
by?
I know that you will take my hand, when the path
comes to its winding end.
I think I shall kiss you, as we sit and make amends.
Will I dream then?
Never more to break and bend.
To the maiden with the lilacs in her hair:.
Death is not the end; I know,
The end is you, my dear.

BELLES

MARIAN

Draw the bow and loose the arrow.
Sheath the sword and wield the hilt.
Carry well your hooded burden;
There's more than one outlaw in Nottingham Wood.

GUINEVERE

Beloved, begotten, bonnie lass.
Wife to a King, mere mistress to a knight.
You change your temper with a flick of the quill,
The ink stains you sweetly, sticks and deems you
mean.
Harlot who deserved less, then the page turns again.
Saintly and chaste dove who would have no other.
Your favour is a rose bud, now a thorn that stabs
righteous hearts.
At the mercy of the draughtsman is your masqued
portrayal.
But to me, My Lady, you are the loveliest.
I bow to you and crown you thus-
Guinevere, Queen of my heart.

MADONNA

Mother to all of us.
Beacon of eternal kindness.
Lady of sorrows.
Queen of the skies.
Matron of candles.
It is to you I pray when I am in pieces.

DAGON'S MUSE

I had a vision of my masterpiece; something to rival
one of Lovecraft's beasts.
She scowled at the words and said she hated it.
My wife had always frowned at my writing methods—
She swore that it wasn't healthy to seclude myself.
My deadlines may press down upon me, but I should
not lose my touch with reality.
My family would embrace me and I should hold
them tightly.
I laughed and told her that reality would still be
there when my work was done.
She did not take it kindly.
She flicked her cigarette onto the pages, and before I
could move, they were ablaze.
For twenty years, she said, she'd worked so that I
could write.
Chained to her office desk, her dreams lost beneath
piles of spreadsheets and paperweights.
For a moment, she watched me struggle; then, she
was gone,
Leaving me nothing but my solitude and my
magnum opus in ashes.
I understood, at last, why she had hated the story, so.
Dagon was a god, once,
A god of the harvest, and everybody loved him.
But what is he known as now?
A monster, who fathered more,
Plucked from his plough and tossed into the sea.
Alone and forgotten.
Feared and reviled.

FAKE VENUS

Tender moonlight in her hair.
From the sea, she calls.
Saturn's light in her eyes; what a pretty, faux disguise.
Jupiter was in her smile, I sat back for a while.
What a pretty, faux disguise for the mistress of lies.

Fake Venus from the stars.
Fake Venus in my heart.
Fake Venus, tearing me, tearing me, tearing me
apart.

Neptune's waters were her playground;
Mars' fires were her toys.
The universe fell to nothing, when she bade it
destroyed.
She looked at me, just a human, and I felt so small.
What a pretty, faux disguise for the master of lies.

Fake Venus, from the stars.
Fake Venus, in my heart.
Fake Venus, tearing me, tearing me, tearing me
apart.

Mercury was in her laughter;
Pluto's gems in her hands.
She turned away into the ocean and left me stranded
on land.

Fake Venus from the stars.
Fake Venus, in my heart.
Fake Venus, tearing me, tearing me, tearing me.
Tearing me apart.

CASSANDRA

Scourged by the sun,
Torn from your home,
Fair, wronged dreamer—
A god gave you sight unseen.
To tempt you, then strike you down.
By man's hands you suffered.
Your end was wrought cruelly
By another wronged damosel.
Rest well, sweet Princess.
This simple song is for thee.

GALATEA

Imperfectly perfect creation:
Made to be loved, to be cradled.
Your origin is steeped in loneliness,
Begged to life by an artist,
Given breath by a goddess.
Will marriage suit you?
Or will you long to return to the mortar?
A stony heart cannot feel tenderness,
Nor can it be torn apart from needing.
I hope he is worthy of you.

ATHENA AND ARES

Radiant Athena sat at her loom with her beloved owl on her shoulder. She spun the fine thread of the vine and wove starlight into delicate fabric. For her craft, she had few rivals.

As she rested her paddle and spindle down beside her, she felt a familiar presence and sensed a visitor. There, in the courtyard, helmet in arm and clad in his glinted armour, stood war-god Ares.

Her owl took wing and found respite on a nearby olive tree, she stood, and the two bowed to each other.

Their lord father, amorous and mighty Zeus, was lord of the skies; the rites of hospitality were always to be upheld, even among the Gods.

After they had broken bread and drank of the sweet Ambrosia, they began to take up a discussion.

Different in nature, their commonality lay in the wars of men. At first, they toasted to victories taken; then, the commendations turned into a fierce debate.

Ares stood for strength, ferocity; the better force would always win, he said.

Athena, meanwhile, upheld that war was nothing without strategy.

Both cited numerous battles throughout time to aid their cause, but they were soon at a stalemate.

Shaking hands in agreement, the two decided to summon an outside force to help break their steely debate. With a quick breath, Ares sounded into his great war horn. After a moment, four glowing figures descended from the astral plane and entered the residence.

There, ever-youthful Apollo stood, his lyre clasped in his hands. A circlet of gold leaf and sunlight sat on his head. He was fearsome and beautiful to behold; all present were in awe.

At her brother's right was Artemis, the great mistress of the hunt. Her face was framed with gentle moonlight, and her forehead bore the Pleiades themselves for a crown.

At Apollo's left side in a shroud of light, was Helios, the Titan of the sun, still mounted in his glorious chariot and clad in cloth of gold.

To Helios's left stood fair Selene, the Titan of the moon and spouse of the eternally- slumbering Endymion. Wife to a Shepherd king as well as a Goddess, she draped herself in silver silk.

-Thine are each other's opposite, in nature and in duty.
Apollo, brother and equal in law;
Artemis, mistress of the bow and hunt,
Golden Helios, the sun's carrier,
And Eternal Selene, the moon's light.
We have called you hence to be the judges-.

Cups of flowing Ambrosia and a modest feast were
shared between them.
Once the meal ended, the two gods took the floor to
speak their case, and Apollo began the discussion.

*-Be warned, cousins, that we may not find an answer.
We see all from above and thus, we are often
withdrawn-*

Ares placed his helmet back on his head and made
his case.

*-Athena is held for strategy, but I am war itself;
the bloody act, the sword which cuts the flesh.
Without me there is naught but talk at a table, no
great victory to promenade. Men who sit in marbled
amphitheatres squirm at my methods, yet all the
same they pray for me to slay their enemies, and to
you, great sister, they pray for wisdom so that they
may butcher their enemies graciously-*

In a harsh tone, Athena gave her rebuttal:

*-Without strategy or wisdom, war is just brutality,
dogs fighting over meat-.*

Though hot-tempered, Ares was careful with his
chides.

*-War is brutality, sister; I think you have been at your
loom too long.-*

-It is better to make something fine than to leave little but scorched earth.- The eternal maid proclaimed.

-Athens would be a second drowned Atlantis if I had let our uncle have his way-

-What is cleverness when a sword is before your throat?-
Swore red-blooded Ares.

-It is the quick thought to turn your sword to your enemy before you are harmed- Athena answered.

The light of their guests shone from her helmet, and in the distance, her Owl sang softly.

-The heat of the battle is not the end of a fight. Without strategy, or forethought, the battalion has no formation, nor do the leaders know what to do when facing their enemies at the table.
War is the foundation of the future for mortal men, and without wisdom, there is no future-.

The luminous beings of the sun and moon whispered among themselves. As Apollo had begun the proceedings, Artemis rose and closed them.

-You are both in tandem.
The very thing that causes you to squabble, you both take great pride in.-

*-War to you is a fine art; it is your essence, but the
worship you are given is because men look to you for
strength and wisdom.
You are the ones who make it a grand affair;
Without you to steer the hands and guide the helm,
mortals would merely crash against each other for
eternity and war would not be worth discussing.
As the moon cannot be without the sun, the strategist
cannot make their ambitions without a soldier to
wield the sword, and the warrior cannot go to war
without first learning who he must fight.-*

At the conclusion, all bowed, and the lunar and solar
deities once again departed in their magnificence.
Athena and Ares regarded each other, and finding
nothing more to say, bade one another farewell.

Acknowledgements

I must, of course, thank my mother, my family, and my partner, without whom I would never have put pen to paper. For their years of encouragement I am eternally grateful.

There are also my wonderful friends, who know who they are and who fill my life with joy.

It would be remiss of me to not mention my many teachers, both those within academia and outside of school hours, who nourished my interests.

Special thanks to the lovely staff at AOS Publishing, who saw something special in these pages and gave me this opportunity.

And, above all, I thank you, dear reader, for giving this the time of day.

May we meet again soon.

Orla Jane Drummond.